What I Eat

At the Fish Hut

By Cecilia Minden

We like the Fish Hut.

We have fun at the Fish Hut.

We all like fish.

We all like corn on the cob.

I like fish sticks.

I get fish sticks and
corn on the cob.

Mom likes crab cakes.

Mom gets crab cakes and corn on the cob.

Dad likes clams.

Dad gets clams and
corn on the cob.

 We have fun at the Fish Hut.

We like the Fish Hut.

Word List

sight words

and	have	to
are	I	We
cakes	like	
corn	the	

short a words	short e words	short i words	short o words	short u words
all	get	Fish	cob	fun
at	gets	sticks	Mom	Hut
clams			on	
crab				
Dad				

72 Words

We like the Fish Hut.
We have fun at the Fish Hut.
We all like fish.
We all like corn on the cob.
I like fish sticks.
I get fish sticks and corn on the cob.
Mom likes crab cakes.
Mom gets crab cakes and corn on the cob.
Dad likes clams.
Dad gets clams and corn on the cob.
We have fun at the Fish Hut.
We like the Fish Hut.

Published in the United States of America by Cherry Lake Publishing
Ann Arbor, Michigan
www.cherrylakepublishing.com

Photo Credits: © gmnicholas/iStockphoto, cover, 1, 11; © junyanjiang/Shutterstock.com, back cover, 10, 15; © zcw/Shutterstock.com, cover, 1, 7, 11; © EAGiven/iStockphoto, 2, 13 – editorial; © LightField Studios/Shutterstock.com, 3, 12; © AS Food studio/Shutterstock.com, 4; © bogdandimages/Shutterstock.com, 5; © Kirill Aleksandrovich/Shutterstock.com, 6; © Kwangmoozaa/Shutterstock.com, 7; © LauriPatterson/iStockphoto, 8; © msheldrake/Can Stock Photo, 9

Cherry Blossom Press is an imprint of Cherry Lake Publishing.

Library of Congress Cataloging-in-Publication Data has been filed and is available at catalog.loc.gov

Printed in the United States of America
Corporate Graphics

Cecilia Minden is the former director of the Language and Literacy Program at Harvard Graduate School of Education. She earned her PhD in Reading Education at the University of Virginia. Dr. Minden has written extensively for early readers. She is passionate about matching children to the very book they need to improve their skills and progress to a deeper understanding of all the wonder books can hold. Dr. Minden and her family live in McKinney, Texas.

CHERRY BLOSSOM PRESS